COUNTDOWN TO SPACE

ASTRONAUTS
Training for Space

Michael D. Cole

Series Advisor:
John E. McLeaish
Chief, Public Information Office, retired,
NASA Johnson Space Center

Enslow Publishers, Inc.

44 Fadem Road	PO Box 38
Box 699	Aldershot
Springfield, NJ 07081	Hants GU12 6BP
USA	UK

Library of Congress Cataloging-in-Publication Data

Cole, Michael D.
    Astronauts : training for space / Michael D. Cole.
       p. cm. — (Countdown to space)
    Includes bibliographical references and index.
    Summary: Describes the qualities needed to be part of the space
program and various aspects of the training that astronaut candidates
receive to prepare them for their first flight.
    ISBN: 0-7660-1116-X
    1. Astronauts—Training of—Juvenile literature.
[1. Astronauts.] I. Title. II. Series
TL850.C64   1999
629.45'07—dc21   98-3299
                                    CIP
                                     AC

Illustration Credits: National Aeronautics and Space Administration (NASA).

Cover Illustration: NASA (foreground); Raghvendra Sahai and John Trauger (JPL),
the WFPC2 science team, NASA, and AURA/STSCI (background).

CONTENTS

Astronaut candidate Dr. Ellen Ochoa is pulled behind a moving vehicle to learn what it feels like to parachute out of an airplane in an emergency.

1

The Right Stuff

Sally Ride was training very hard to be an astronaut in August 1978. In the middle of a three-day ocean survival exercise, she was still four years away from becoming the first American woman in space.

That day was neither historic nor glamorous for the future astronaut. Ride was bobbing about in a rubber raft in the choppy waters off the southern tip of Florida. She was cold and wet, and she was beginning to realize how tough her training was going to be.

"What am I doing here?" Ride asked herself as she shivered in the cold ocean waters. "I'm supposed to be a *smart* person."[1]

Sally Ride, an astrophysicist, was smart enough to

know one thing for certain—the training was not going to get easier.

Before the three days were over, Ride and her fellow trainees were hooked by rope to a motorboat and dragged backward through Biscayne Bay. They made four-hundred-foot parachute jumps into the ocean. They swung down from a forty-five-foot tower into water infested with mosquitoes.

Some of the training was fun. There was the first day she flew in the special KC-135 aircraft nicknamed the "vomit comet."

The plane would climb and dive in a way that would leave the astronauts floating freely in the cargo bay. This gave the astronauts their first experience with microgravity, or the feeling of weightlessness. Most of the astronauts enjoyed that part, although it did tend to make them queasy.

Shannon Lucid was another astronaut in training with Sally Ride. Ride became the first American woman in space. Lucid was preparing for her own great accomplishment in space years later.

Lucid remembers being dragged along a dusty road behind a motorcycle to show her what it would be like to be dragged by a parachute. She practiced squirming out of a spacecraft in the ocean and jumping into a wave-tossed sea. She was spun around in a circle by a machine called a centrifuge. This tested her endurance of the

Nancy J. Sherlock, wearing flight coveralls and a helmet, holds onto her parachute harness in preparation for parachute drag training.

pressures, or g-forces, astronauts experience during liftoff and reentry into Earth's atmosphere.[2]

Eighteen years later, in October 1996, the space shuttle *Atlantis* landed at the Kennedy Space Center in Florida. When the hatch was opened, Shannon Lucid walked down the steps from the shuttle to the landing strip. Lucid had just returned from spending a record 188 days in orbit aboard the Russian *Mir* space station.[3] At that time, most astronauts who had spent more than one hundred days in space had great trouble standing or walking when they returned to Earth. Being weightless in space can usually weaken the muscles in people's legs.[4]

But Shannon Lucid had been an astronaut for eighteen years. She had trained hard for all five of her missions into space. This time Lucid had made the extra effort to continue her physical training *during* the long mission. The sight of Lucid walking down the steps from the shuttle proved that all her training had paid off.

Maybe you have what it takes to become an astronaut. Let's look at some of the basic qualities every astronaut must have.

Every astronaut must be in good physical condition. Perfect vision or hearing is not required, but an astronaut's body needs to be strong, sturdy, and physically fit. The stress of g-forces during liftoff and reentry takes a toll on the body, as does the effect of prolonged weightlessness. For these reasons, it can be an unpleasant and dangerous experience for anyone not in top physical condition.

Astronauts need to be hard workers. As shown by

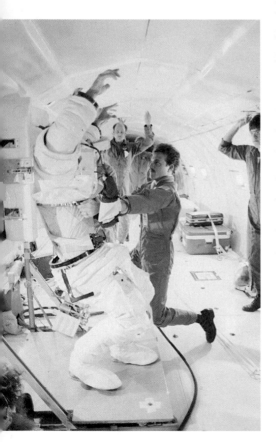

Crew members participate in suiting exercises aboard the KC-135 aircraft.

the experiences of Shannon Lucid, getting into space involves a tremendous amount of preparation. Many physical skills, such as moving about in a space suit, need to be learned. Many technical skills, such as operating the robotic arm in the shuttle's payload bay, need to be mastered.

Astronauts must work well under stress because they often perform under difficult conditions. Equipment aboard the shuttle does not always operate perfectly. If an engine burns out during launch, the astronauts must be ready and able to fly the shuttle to an emergency landing at any of a number of designated landing strips around the world. While in orbit, they must adapt to equipment failures in a way that will allow them to accomplish their mission.

Sally Ride and Shannon Lucid were trained to be mission specialists. Astronaut pilots, who fly the shuttle, are trained differently because they have different responsibilities during a mission. Whether they are mission specialists or astronaut pilots, all astronauts must develop control in stressful situations. A good astronaut learns to never panic, for it may cost someone's life . . . including his or her own.

Space travel itself is a continuous learning experience. Every mission teaches us more about space and how human beings can adapt to it. Shannon Lucid's 188 days in space showed the National Aeronautics and Space Administration (NASA) that frequent, strenuous exercise while in orbit can reduce the weakening of muscles that astronauts usually experience during longer missions. Astronauts never tire of learning. They have much to learn in order to get into space, and they are expected to learn even more once they are there.

If most or all of these qualities describe you, then you may someday have the "right stuff" to become an astronaut. Then you can begin your training.

Astronauts (from left to right) Robert Crippen, Frederick Hauck, John Fabian, and Sally Ride sit in the mission simulator in preparation for launch and landing of their shuttle mission.

2

Basic Astronaut Training

There was a momentary crisis taking place just above the surface of the Moon on July 20, 1969. As Neil Armstrong saw the landing area for his Apollo lunar module come into view, he saw that it was scattered with large boulders. The lunar module's onboard computer was carrying them to a landing amid the boulders. This would almost certainly cause them to crash.

Armstrong quickly took manual control of the module. With his copilot Edwin Aldrin calling out instrument readings to him, and using the handle for the control rockets, Armstrong guided the lunar module over the boulders toward a smoother landing area in the distance.

The spacecraft's fuel was running dangerously close

to empty. The extra distance was not in the plan for the landing. With almost no fuel remaining, Armstrong finally settled the lunar module *Eagle* down on the surface of the Moon.

"The *Eagle* has landed," he said.[1]

The *Eagle* would not have landed if its two astronauts had not trained and prepared for such an emergency. This historic example demonstrates many of the same important qualities required of astronauts in training today. Armstrong and Aldrin performed well under stress. They also performed well as a team. They were aboard the lunar module that day not only because they were good pilots, but also because they were accomplished people in their chosen fields of science and engineering.

Piloting skills will always be a part of the space program. Among today's astronauts, scientific expertise is just as important. The space shuttles that carry astronauts into space today are extremely complex. They require people with high levels of education and training to pilot them and to operate their equipment.

Let's imagine that you have been a military test pilot for years. Or suppose you have a college degree in biology, engineering, or physics. You apply to NASA to become an astronaut and are selected.

NASA expects that you will complete your training successfully (they would not have chosen you if they did not think you could do so), and most people will start

Without the proper emergency training it is possible that Neil Armstrong and Edwin Aldrin would never have walked on the Moon.

thinking of you as an astronaut. But you are not exactly an astronaut yet.

You are an astronaut *candidate* (ASCAN). As a candidate, NASA will assign you to the astronaut office at Johnson Space Center in Houston, Texas. Based on your background, you will train as either an astronaut pilot or a mission specialist. In the early phase, many of the training exercises for both astronaut pilots and mission specialists are the same.

For one year, all astronaut candidates are taught information and trained in the basic skills they will need as astronauts. They go through physical training and learn the shuttle's many systems. The candidates are trained to use equipment such as space suits and the shuttle's robotic arm. This phase of training is designed to show whether or not a candidate is capable of being an astronaut. Each candidate must complete this part of the training successfully before he or she can be chosen as an astronaut for a specific mission. At the same time, each candidate must prove that he or she is in excellent physical condition through various physical fitness tests.

"We literally ran until we couldn't run anymore," said astronaut Mary Cleave. "They tested our strength, and generally made sure we were healthy. Then, once we were selected, it was up to us to stay at that level of fitness."[2]

During astronaut candidate training, the candidates are first exposed to microgravity in the vomit comet. The modified KC-135 aircraft climbs to 32,000 feet, then dives in an arc to 25,000 feet. This controlled arc causes the astronauts to float up off the floor, creating a feeling of weightlessness inside the plane. Then the plane begins its climb again, and again it dives. During a normal training session aboard the vomit comet, this up-and-down process is repeated as many as forty times. This is a good test of the astronaut candidates' stomachs.[3]

During these brief periods of weightlessness, the trainees practice eating and drinking. They also practice using some of the small equipment and tools they will use aboard the shuttle.[4]

Astronauts have to be prepared for all kinds of emergencies. They spend many hours in aircraft during their training. They need to know what to do if something goes wrong with the training aircraft. On space missions, if there is a dangerous shuttle malfunction during certain phases of launch or reentry, they may have to bail out of the shuttle. They do this by deploying a long, curved pole from the side of the shuttle near an escape door. The astronauts, wearing parachutes, open the door and place a hook attached to their suit onto the pole. They then jump out of the shuttle. The hook causes them to slide down and then off the end of

the pole. The pole ensures that the parachuting astronauts get clear of the shuttle and will not be carried back to collide with the shuttle wing or tail rudder.

Once the astronauts bail out, they must know how to come down safely. When their descent is over, they must know how to survive, whether they come down on

Astronaut Shannon Lucid descends safely to the ground during emergency escape training.

land or in water. To prepare for these situations, astronaut candidates are given survival training.

Emergencies may occur shortly before launch. A leak in one of the solid rocket boosters could cause an explosion. If a leak occurs, the astronauts must evacuate the launchpad. Candidates practice exiting the shuttle orbiter and climbing into a large steel cage. The cage is connected to a very long cable anchored to the ground twelve hundred feet away. When the cage is released, it quickly travels along the cable, away from the launchpad. The cage carries the astronauts away from danger and skids to a stop on the ground.

After they have received instruction in scuba diving, the candidates are trained in the operation of space suits. Further training in weightlessness and in the operation of the suits is done in the neutral buoyancy tank. This tank, officially called the Neutral Buoyancy Lab (NBL), is a special forty-foot-deep water tank at Johnson Space Center in Houston. It holds 6.2 million gallons of water. The tank is so large that a full-scale mock-up of the shuttle can fit inside it.

Submerged in the tank, astronaut candidates experience what it would feel like to float in microgravity outside the shuttle in a pressurized space suit. They also discover whether or not they have the coordination skills to work in that strange environment. Astronaut Jack Lousma, commander of the second *Skylab* crew in the mid-1970s, who later flew aboard the

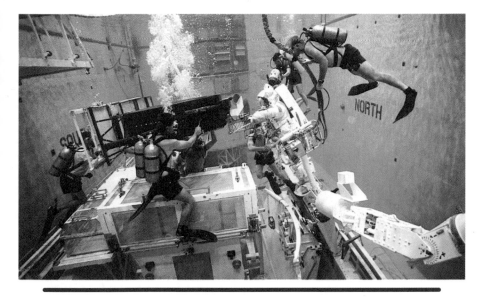

Astronaut Thomas Akers (in white) trains in the Neutral Buoyancy Lab. The underwater exercise prepares astronauts for their work in the weightless environment of space.

shuttle, used a similar tank to prepare for his space walks.

"If you can do it in the water tank, you can do it in zero gravity," he said. "It's a great training and development tool." While conducting his first walk in space, Lousma enthusiastically said to the controllers in Houston, "It's just like the tank . . . only deeper."[5]

Preparing the astronaut candidates' minds for space is as important as preparing their bodies. The candidates spend hours in classrooms taking science and technical courses. Some of the classes are in mathematics, Earth resources, meteorology, guidance and navigation, astronomy, physics, and computer sciences.

Astronaut candidates must know how the shuttle works before they can fly aboard it. They read many books and technical manuals and attend lectures about the shuttle systems. Although not all the astronauts will actually pilot the shuttle, they all need to understand its systems inside and out.

As their training progresses, astronaut candidates go to work in the Shuttle Mission Simulator (SMS). This mock-up of the orbiter trains the candidates for what it will be like to work, live, eat, and sleep aboard the shuttle. The controls and displays of the SMS are connected to computers designed to make the simulator react exactly as the real shuttle would. The simulator, however, cannot show astronauts what it will be like without gravity.

The computer also throws problems at the trainees. The simulated problems test the candidates' knowledge of the shuttle, as well as their abilities to think and work as a team. It gives the astronauts important practice in how to react to malfunctions or crises aboard the shuttle.[6]

The space shuttle lands on a runway much like any other aircraft. But the shuttle is big and lands at twice the speed of a commercial airliner. It also sets down on the runway in what is called a deadstick landing. This means that it glides down to the runway without any power from its engines. The pilot who lands it must control the shuttle with great skill to glide the huge bird down without power.

Astronaut candidates who will pilot the shuttle practice these skills in special training aircraft. The T-38 is a small, high-performance jet aircraft that the astronaut pilots use to keep their flying skills sharp. These planes are also frequently used by the astronauts to transport themselves to and from the various space centers for different parts of their training.

A four-engine KC-135 gives the astronauts experience in flying large, heavy aircraft. It gives them a good idea

The T-38 is the special training aircraft that astronaut pilots use to keep their flying skills sharp.

of how the shuttle will feel as it descends through the atmosphere.

When you have successfully completed this year of basic astronaut training, you will become a regular member of the astronaut corps. Now you are officially an astronaut!

But your training is far from over. Normally at least one more year of training is needed before you will become eligible for your first mission assignment.[7]

Sometimes it is longer. You continue on to advanced training. New knowledge and skills are learned to make yourself ready for that exciting day when NASA assigns you to your first space mission.

3

Advanced Training

Sally Ride was good at almost everything she did, from astrophysics to playing tennis. By the time she had moved into her advanced phase of astronaut training, it looked as if she would be a good astronaut, too.

But she had never before worked with a robot.

Part of Ride's advanced training as a mission specialist included intense work on the shuttle's Remote Manipulator System (RMS). The RMS is the long robotic arm astronauts use to move large objects, such as satellites, in and out of the shuttle's payload bay. Ride spent many long hours training to use the RMS. She practiced until she was able to pick up small, delicate objects, as well as larger, more bulky equipment.

"It got to be as natural as using tweezers on a

noodle," she said, laughing. "I began to think that all there was to being an astronaut was launching an arm."[1]

Many different tasks must be accomplished aboard a space shuttle, and astronauts are trained to become specialized in certain areas. This advanced training depends on the astronaut's flight experience and scientific background. The three kinds of astronauts are astronaut pilots, mission specialists, and payload specialists.

Astronaut pilots fly the space shuttles or other spacecraft. They may also serve as mission commanders. Their background is in flying jet aircraft, usually as military test pilots. Eyesight and physical fitness

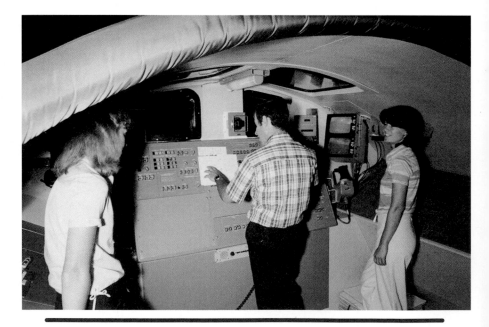

Inside the Remote Manipulator System simulator, Terry Hart (left) and Sally Ride (right) familiarize themselves with the robotic arm.

requirements for astronaut pilots are stricter than for mission and payload specialists.[2]

Much of the astronaut pilots' advanced training is focused on flying and commanding the shuttle. Pilots spend a great amount of time in computerized flight simulators. The simulators train them in every step of the shuttle's flight operations—from liftoff to orbit, reentry, and landing.

Astronaut pilots also train for many, many hours in the flight training aircraft. They work especially hard in the Grumman Gulfstream II. This aircraft simulates the feeling of the shuttle's deadstick landing. A successful landing is such an important part of the mission that astronaut pilots practice this skill to perfection.

Mission specialists are trained to perform various experiments and technical tasks in space. These astronauts all have advanced degrees in science or engineering. They are responsible, along with the mission commander, for coordinating work and activities aboard the shuttle during missions.[3] They perform onboard experiments and are involved in space walks. Mission specialists are concerned with the shuttle's payload operations. Because of this, mission specialists are trained in using the RMS.[4]

Advanced training for mission specialists includes more practice in spacewalking and in performing experiments aboard shuttle simulators. Simulators also

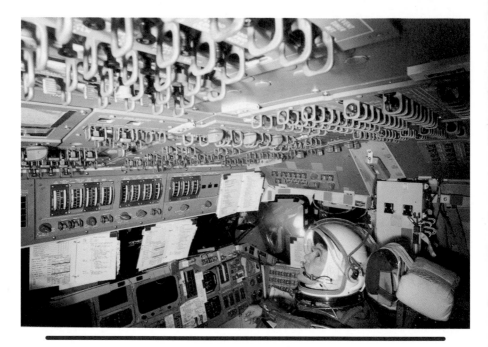

Robert Cabana is seated at the pilot's station of the Shuttle Mission Simulator. He is surrounded by checklists, control panels, and various onboard equipment.

train these astronauts how to use and monitor the shuttle's supplies, such as fuel, water, and food.

Payload specialists are trained to perform specific experiments on a particular shuttle flight. They usually work for the company that has paid NASA to fly an experiment or a satellite payload aboard the shuttle. Companies prefer to have one of their own experts in space to oversee their payloads. Payload specialists are not full-time astronauts like the others. They must go through training similar to mission specialists, however, before they may go into space. The rest of their training is focused on their particular payload.

Some training is shared by astronaut pilots, mission specialists, and payload specialists. Although mission specialists do not learn how to fly the shuttle and pilots do not learn all the details of how to conduct experiments, all the astronauts should have a broad understanding of their mission and work together as a team.

During actual shuttle missions, pilot and mission specialist trainees spend time working as capsule

Astronaut trainees serve as spacecraft communicators to become familiar with a real shuttle flight. Here, Drs. William and Anna Fisher (husband and wife) monitor a shuttle flight from the capcom console.

communicators, or capcoms, at Mission Control. Capcoms communicate with the astronauts on the shuttle. Serving as capcoms helps the astronaut trainees become more familiar with the workings of a real shuttle flight.

Pilots and mission specialists continue to train for space walks in the Neutral Buoyancy Lab (NBL). "The biggest part of the training for these space walks is done in the water," said astronaut Leroy Chiao, referring to the NBL. During sessions in the huge tank, the astronauts are submerged underwater in their space suits for up to six hours at a time.

"It's a very simple concept really," Chiao explained. "We have these mock-ups made that mimic the payload bay and the hardware we're going to be using. In this way we can simulate that we're in space and actually doing the tasks that we'll be performing."[5]

Pilots and mission specialists are also trained in using the Simplified Aid For Extravehicular activity Rescue (SAFER) unit. SAFER is a backpack device with thruster jets that can propel an astronaut through space during a space walk. The astronaut controls the backpack by moving an attached joystick. Moving the joystick in various directions will propel the astronaut forward or backward, up or down, or from side to side. It will tilt him at any angle she or he wishes to be.

Some of the most important work done by the astronauts must be done outside their spacecraft. The

Leroy Chiao is ready to enter the neutral buoyancy tank. He will practice underwater with mock-ups of the equipment and hardware that will be used on his shuttle mission.

SAFER unit was designed primarily as a safety device in case an astronaut gets loose during a space walk.

Construction of the International Space Station will require a tremendous number of hours for space walks. A faulty turn against some equipment in the payload bay during a space walk could tear a hole in the astronaut's space suit. Such a crisis would give the astronaut little time to return to the airlock before the suit loses pressure and the person runs out of air to breathe.

Emergencies such as these are the reasons that practice for space walks is long and exhaustive. One mistake in space could cost an astronaut his or her life. The goal of training is to minimize these dangers.

As the months go by, your training continues. You are trained to use the RMS. In two missions to repair the Hubble Space Telescope, the RMS pulled the telescope into the payload bay of the shuttle. To make the delicate repairs, an astronaut was strapped to the end of the robotic arm and moved carefully around the telescope by the RMS operator inside the shuttle.

After months and months of training, you gradually begin to feel you have a good understanding of the shuttle and its systems. You have served as a capcom at Mission Control. You have become skilled in the space walk training tank, and you understand how to use the SAFER unit.

Now comes the big news. You have been assigned to your first shuttle mission. Although astronauts are trained to stay cool, few of them can contain their excitement when they learn they have been assigned to a mission. Winston Scott, an astronaut assigned to his first shuttle flight on mission STS-72 in 1996, was elated. The first thing he did was telephone his wife with the news.

"They just announced the '72 crew, and yours truly is on it," he said beaming. "That's really something, isn't it!"[6]

Your entire crew of astronauts has been named and your mission is scheduled to launch a year and a half from now. You learn that your mission is to launch one satellite from the payload bay. You are to retrieve another satellite from orbit, repair it, then rerelease it into orbit. Several experiments will also be conducted aboard the shuttle.

Now that your crew is assembled and the goals for your mission are set, your training becomes focused on the specific tasks of your mission. Your entire crew begins training together in the SMS.[7]

There are actually two SMS systems. One is connected to machines that move the cockpit to simulate the flight motions astronauts command it to make. The other simulates payload activities, especially the movements of the remote manipulator arm. It is here that your crew practices launching one satellite and guiding the other satellite in for repair.

As the time for the mission draws nearer, you do long-duration training inside the SMS. You eat and sleep

Pilot Kent Rominger (left) views a monitor displaying underwater extravehicular activity rehearsal of his crewmates.

aboard the simulator for days, just as you would aboard the shuttle.[8]

"We'll be trying to assimilate the entire flight in advance by computer," Dr. Sally Ride told a reporter before one of her missions. "This is intense training. We'll aim to be prepared for anything that might come up."[9]

Training for space walks, or extravehicular activities, becomes very specific to the mission. In the NBL, you begin practicing with the tools you will use to repair the satellite. A full-scale mock-up of the satellite is put into the tank to assist you.

When the launch is only a few days away, your shuttle will have been rolled out on the giant-tracked platform. The platform carries the upright spacecraft on its slow, three-mile journey to the launchpad. Like you, the spacecraft is waiting to blast off into space. Still you practice and train.

You and your crew climb

Astronaut Story Musgrave poses in front of Discovery *at the 195-foot level elevator entrance to the launchpad.*

aboard a van and are driven to the launchpad. You ride an elevator up to the shuttle's hatch. Technicians help you climb inside the shuttle and strap you into your seat. You can hear the countdown in your helmet. You cannot help feeling the excitement as it comes down to the final seconds.

But it is only a rehearsal.

Every detail of the countdown is practiced. This helps NASA discover any problems with the shuttle and fix them before the actual launch. The procedures test communications and allow all crew members to practice their responsibilities during launch.

Astronaut Frederick Gregory had trained many times on the launchpad. After a while he felt very comfortable, even when there were interruptions in the countdown and he needed to wait patiently for practice to resume. "I was so confident," he said, "that when I got on board, and there were any breaks, I just shut my eyes and drifted off."[10] Gregory's confidence was the confidence built by training.

Finally your training for this mission is over. It is time for the real thing. Before you go to bed, you check the countdown.

T minus twelve hours . . . and counting.

The big day is almost here. Tomorrow morning you will put all your training to use when you soar for the first time into space.

4
Ready for Liftoff

You wake up in your bed. It feels almost like any other morning, with lots of training ahead. But this is not just another morning.

Today you are going into space. Today is launch day!

The fact that it almost feels like any other morning is an important point. Although you are excited, you are familiar with everything that is happening. You have done it before. You have gotten up and dressed in your flight suit. You have stepped into the van to ride to the pad. You have climbed into the shuttle and waited through the countdown.

Your training and practice have put you at ease with everything that is happening. You have practiced all of it.

Seeing it work in practice has made you confident that it will work again today.

Still, you *are* thrilled!

"I was pretty excited," said astronaut Charles Bolden about the hours before his first mission. "I don't think I had any undue concern. You're trained. We all felt very comfortable, confident. But I was concerned about being able to do my job if something unusual came up."[1]

After eating breakfast with your crew, you step into the van that carries you to the pad. You ride the elevator to the shuttle's hatch. One by one you and your crew climb into the shuttle. You put on your helmets. The technicians help strap you and your crewmates into your seats. Several minutes later the technicians leave the shuttle. One of your crewmates reaches over and seals the hatch. The technicians remain outside to conduct leak tests on the hatch. When they are certain that it is sealed, they leave the pad.

You are lying on your back

Seven crew members leave the Operations and Checkout Building to board a van headed for the launchpad.

facing up toward the sky. The commander is in the left front seat. The pilot is in the right front seat. You, a mission specialist, are seated directly behind the pilot. Another mission specialist sits to your left, behind the commander. Behind you, two more mission specialists and a payload specialist are strapped in their seats on the mid deck.

You hear the sounds of the countdown in your helmet. It moves into the final minute, then the final seconds. *Ten . . . nine . . . eight . . . seven . . . six . . . We have Go for main engine start.* You hear the engines rumble below. The shuttle begins to shake. *Four . . . three . . . two . . . one . . . Liftoff!*

Suddenly you feel the shuttle surge into the sky. Even through your helmet, the sound of the engines and the solid rocket boosters is deafening. The spacecraft vibrates as it rockets higher and higher, faster and faster. The commander and pilot communicate with launch control, until communication is switched over to Mission Control in Houston.

"You are Go at throttle up," you hear the capcom say from Houston. The shuttle's increasing speed presses you back into your seat.

The solid rocket boosters separate and the ride suddenly becomes very smooth. Minutes later the large external tank is jettisoned. The shuttle has rocketed into orbit.

When Mission Control confirms that the shuttle is in

orbit, you remove your helmet and unfasten your straps. Your body floats up off the seat. You are in microgravity—this time for real!

The shuttle payload bay doors are opened. The doors have heat radiators that must be exposed to space to vent the heat from the shuttle. Keeping the payload bay doors closed would cause the orbiter to overheat.[2]

Gradually you and your crew adjust to the sensation of being in space. You and your crewmates conduct a number of experiments. You eat and sleep aboard the shuttle. Except for the microgravity, everything seems very much like it was in the simulator.

After hearing the countdown through their helmets, astronauts inside the shuttle will hear the engines rumble as liftoff begins.

Eventually the time comes to prepare for the satellite retrieval operation. The pilot flies the shuttle into position near the ailing satellite. The commander takes his place at the payload bay windows. He is beside the mission specialist who will control the remote manipulator arm. From there, the commander will coordinate the operation. The commander will communicate with Mission Control and give instructions to the pilot.

Very gently, the mission specialist grasps the satellite with the RMS. Using slow and careful movements of the controls, the mission specialist settles the satellite into the payload bay.

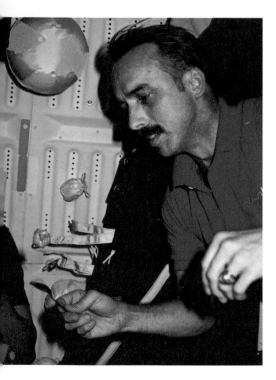

Now it is your turn to perform. You and your spacewalking partner enter the airlock. In spite of all your training in the NBL, you are nervous about venturing out into space for the first time.

The hatch opens. Outside the open payload bay, Earth is huge and beautiful. You remember that you are there

Astronaut James Adamson enjoys the rare opportunity of eating in a weightless environment as he flips a shrimp with a spoon.

to do a job, so you slowly guide yourself out of the airlock and into the open payload bay. It is a terrific, exhilarating experience. You are now more excited than nervous.

After taking a few minutes to adjust to the sensation of being weightless in the suit outside the shuttle, you focus your mind on the business at hand. Doing everything as you had done in the NBL, you grab your tools and move carefully toward the satellite. You open the panels on the satellite and begin to do your repairs. Once you get busy, you become very relaxed, just as you did in the water tank. You encounter a problem or two with the repairs, but your training has prepared you for them, and you quickly fix them.

When you are nearly finished, you encounter another problem. The panels on the satellite will not close. Your training has not prepared you for this. It has, however, prepared you to think clearly in such a situation. You decide to use a tool called a come-along, which will pull both sides of the panel shut at the same time. You attach the tool to both of the panels and slowly pull them together until they shut. It works![3]

With your job completed, the two of you return to the airlock. Later a mission specialist uses the RMS to lift the satellite out and away from the shuttle. Finally the arm releases the repaired satellite, sending it back into orbit. You have done it!

A few days later your shuttle returns to Earth. You

are proud that your mission, including your difficult space walk, has been a huge success. The years of training that you and everyone on your crew have put into the mission have all been worth it. You can hardly wait to do it again.

Being an astronaut is hard work. But there is no doubt that it is exciting. What can you, a young person, do right now to prepare yourself for a career in space exploration?

First, you should enjoy math, science, and technology. Math and science can unlock the mysteries of the universe. Without these fields, human beings would never have understood space, let alone gotten there.

Learn all that you can. Everything you learn in school, including music, art, and languages, will help you in a space-related career. Outside of school, scouting and sports activities will also prove useful. One of the most important qualities for astronauts and others in the space program is curiosity.[4] You need to be curious about everything. It is not enough to simply know about space. Knowing about people, cultures, languages, and other subjects will not only make you a better astronaut, but also make you a better person in whatever field you choose to pursue.

Discover the infinite resources of computers. There are many computer programs dealing with space and space travel that are both interesting and fun. These

Astronaut Ronald Sega, center, shares the airlock of the space shuttle Atlantis *with Linda Godwin and Michael Clifford.*

programs can be great learning tools for people interested in space.

Find out if your computer is connected to the Internet. If it is, you can access space-related information from NASA and other space organizations. You can get the latest news on current space missions. Sometimes you can send questions to the astronauts. You can even download the latest photos of distant galaxies from NASA's Hubble Space Telescope.

Discover the fun of model rockets and amateur astronomy. Model rocketry is an enjoyable hobby that will instruct you in the simpler principles of rocket science. Astronomy is another hobby that will help give you a greater understanding of the planets, the stars, and the universe.

If you are interested in doing experiments, you might want to find out about science fairs. Science fairs are competitions where young people display experimental science projects. Your parents or teachers can guide you on how to do science projects. They can also tell you where and how to enter your project in science fairs.

Space Camp is a special camp for young people that gives you a taste of astronaut training. It is a tremendous experience for anyone interested in a space career. The two U.S. Space Camps are located in Huntsville, Alabama, and at the Kennedy Space Center in Florida. Your teachers or school librarian can help you find information about Space Camp.

Young Astronauts is a club you can join. After joining the club, you will receive space-related books, materials, and projects through the mail. If you complete some of these projects you can move up to higher levels of the club. If you are interested, use your library or the Internet to find out more about Young Astronauts.

Your city or county may also have a planetarium. A planetarium is a domed building that uses a special machine to project images of the night sky upon its curved ceiling. Planetariums are used to teach people about astronomy and space.

You can start preparing now for a future career in space.

For those who have already been to space and back, space is more exciting now than when they dreamed of it as children.

"I believe in spaceflight," said astronaut Story Musgrave in 1997, after six shuttle missions and thirty years as a NASA astronaut. "I believe that the kinds of things we discover during spaceflight are very important to humanity, because [they help] us to discover what it means to be human, and what our place in this universe is."[5]

Space *is* exciting. And you can begin training for your future in space today.

CHAPTER NOTES

Chapter 1. The Right Stuff

1. Karen O'Conner, *Sally Ride and the New Astronauts: Scientists in Space* (New York: Franklin Watts, 1983), p. 1.

2. Sharon Begley, "Down to Earth," *Newsweek*, October 7, 1996, p. 32.

3. Ibid., p. 30.

4. Valerie Neal, Cathleen S. Lewis, and Frank H. Winter, *Spaceflight: A Smithsonian Guide* (New York: Macmillan, 1995), p. 19.

Chapter 2. Basic Astronaut Training

1. *Apollo 11, Technical Air-to-Ground Voice Transcription*, Manned Spacecraft Center, Houston, Texas, July 1969.

2. Karen O'Conner, *Sally Ride and the New Astronauts: Scientists in Space* (New York: Franklin Watts, 1983), p. 54.

3. NASA, "Selection and Training of Astronauts," *Information Summaries*, August 1993, <http://shuttle.nasa.gov/sts-74/factshts/asseltrn.html> (June 16, 1998).

4. H. J. P. Arnold, ed., *Man in Space: An Illustrated History of Spaceflight* (New York: Smithmark Publishers, Inc., 1993), p. 133.

5. Mary Virginia Fox, *Women Astronauts: Aboard the Shuttle* (New York: Julian Messner, 1987), p. 108.

6. NASA.

7. Ibid.

Chapter 3. Advanced Training

1. Mary Virginia Fox, *Women Astronauts: Aboard the Shuttle* (New York: Julian Messner, 1987), p. 112.

2. NASA, "Selection and Training of Astronauts," *Information Summaries*, August 1993, <http://shuttle.nasa.gov/sts-74/factshts/asseltrn.html> (June 16, 1998).

3. Michael Rycroft, ed., *Cambridge Encyclopedia of Space* (New York: Cambridge University Press, 1990), p. 258.

4. NASA.

5. PBS Home Video, *Astronauts*, narrated by Bill Nye, 1996.

6. Ibid.

7. NASA.

8. H. J. P. Arnold, ed., *Man in Space: An Illustrated History of Spaceflight* (New York: Smithmark Publishers, Inc., 1993), p. 134.

9. Karen O'Conner, *Sally Ride and the New Astronauts: Scientists in Space* (New York: Franklin Watts, 1983), p. 56.

10. J. Alfred Phelps, *They Had a Dream: The Story of African-American Astronauts* (Novato, Calif.: Presidio Press, 1994), p. 137.

Chapter 4. Ready for Liftoff

1. J. Alfred Phelps, *They Had a Dream: The Story of African-American Astronauts* (Novato, Calif.: Presidio Press, 1994), p. 159.

2. Valerie Neal, Cathleen S. Lewis, and Frank H. Winter, *Spaceflight: A Smithsonian Guide* (New York: Macmillan, 1995), p. 120.

3. NOVA Adventures in Science, *Rescue Mission in Space: The Hubble Space Telescope*, 1994 video.

4. Penelope and Raymond McPhee, Flip and Debra Shulke, *Your Future in Space* (New York: Crown Publishers, Inc., 1986), p. 11.

5. Robert Z. Pearlman, "Ask An Astronaut: Story Musgrave," *Ad Astra*, May–June 1997, p. 22.

GLOSSARY

astronaut pilots—Astronauts responsible for piloting and commanding space shuttle missions.

capcom—Capsule communicator; the person at Mission Control who is responsible for communicating with shuttle astronauts.

centrifuge—A training device that spins astronauts around at high speeds, simulating the g-forces they will experience during liftoff and reentry.

deadstick landing—The landing of an aircraft that is unpowered, such as the gliding space shuttle's unpowered landing after reentry.

deploy—To move an object, such as a satellite, into position.

extravehicular activity—Any human space activity that takes place outside the crew compartments of the space shuttle.

g-force—The force exerted on a person or object caused by a change in acceleration.

Hubble Space Telescope—An orbiting observatory equipped with a very powerful telescope, designed to view objects up to 13 billion light-years away.

International Space Station—A permanent laboratory orbiting Earth that will enable us to conduct long-term research in space. It is the largest international scientific project ever attempted.

jettison—To release or eject something from a spacecraft.

microgravity—The sensation of weightlessness experienced by astronauts in orbit around Earth.

mission specialist—Astronauts primarily responsible for conducting experiments and coordinating payload operations.

Neutral Buoyancy Laboratory (NBL)—Giant water tank that simulates a weightless environment. It allows astronauts to train for space walks.

payload—The cargo, such as satellites, space laboratories, or other equipment, carried aboard the space shuttle.

payload specialist—Astronaut responsible for a particular experiment with the payload aboard a specific space shuttle flight.

Remote Manipulator System (RMS)—System aboard the shuttle that includes a long robotic arm capable of moving large objects in and out of the shuttle's payload bay.

Shuttle Mission Simulator (SMS)—Sophisticated computerized mock-up of the space shuttle that imitates all phases of a shuttle mission, from liftoff to landing.

FURTHER READING

Books

Baird, Anne. *Space Camp: The Great Adventure for NASA Hopefuls.* New York: Morrow Junior Books, 1995.

Cole, Michael D. *Columbia: First Flight of the Space Shuttle.* Springfield, N.J.: Enslow Publishers, Inc., 1995.

Gold, Susan D. *To Space & Back: The Story of the Shuttle.* New York: Crestwood House, 1992.

Kramer, Barbara. *Sally Ride: A Space Biography.* Springfield, N.J.: Enslow Publishers, Inc., 1998.

Maze, Stephanie. *I Want to Be an Astronaut.* San Diego: Harcourt Brace & Company, 1997.

Pogue, William R. *How Do You Go to the Bathroom in Space?* New York: Tor Books, 1991.

Ride, Sally and Susan Okie. *To Space & Back.* New York: Lothrup, Lee & Shepard, 1989.

Sumners, Carolyn. *Toys in Space: Exploring Science with the Astronauts.* New York: The McGraw-Hill Companies, 1997.

Internet Sources

Kansas Cosmosphere and Space Center. "Cosmosphere Future Astronaut Training Program." n.d. <http://www.cosmo.org\astrocamp.htm> (May 28, 1998).

NASA. "International Space Station." n.d. <http://station.nasa.gov> (May 18, 1998).

NASA. "The NASA Shuttle Web." n.d. <http://shuttle.nasa.gov> (May 18, 1998).

NASA. "NASA Spacelink Home." n.d. <http://spacelink.msfc.nasa.gov> (May 18, 1998).

INDEX